WILLIE RUSHTON'S

Great Moments of History

24 ILLUSTRATIONS
IN GLORIOUS COLOUR

D0544153

Published by Charles Herridge Ltd
in association with
the Victoria and Albert Museum
Distributed by Sidgwick & Jackson

© Copyright William Rushton 1984

First published in 1984 by
the Victoria and Albert Museum
in an edition limited to 1,000 copies

This edition published in 1985 by
Charles Herridge Ltd
Woodacott, Northam, Bideford, Devon EX39 1NB

Printed in Italy by New Interlitho SpA, Milan
ISBN 0-946569-10-X

Distributed by Sidgwick & Jackson Ltd
1 Tavistock Chambers, Bloomsbury Way
London WC1A 2SG

FOREWORD

Why, you may ask, is such a venerable institution as the Victoria and Albert Museum publishing a work of Willie Rushton's? The reason is quite simple. While his art may be scandalous, outrageous, even to some obscene, it is the work of a major contemporary satirist. By acquiring the original designs the V&A preserves not just the best of contemporary satirical art but also a piece of social history – for Rushton's work speaks volumes for the way we regard our time and our past.

Rushton is perhaps the most talented of that school that emerged from *Private Eye* in the '60s. His line is clear if eccentric. His work is entirely original. But his satire is always based on a canny likeness. It is the deadliness with which he identifies his target and the precision with which he pinions his victim that has caused the spectator to flinch. And the odd lawsuit. His eagerly awaited cartoons that illustrate Auberon Waugh's page in the Eye, a job he took over from Nicholas Bentley, have been the subject of much shock/horror reaction because of their refusal to respect "good taste" or propriety.

Those who have found Rushton's art distasteful or unkind, particularly when his victim is, like Royalty, somewhat helpless, should bear in mind that it was only in the sanitised age from the later Victorians to the recent past that deference was shown the great or the mighty. Gilray and Rowlandson and Cruickshank were far freer with their scorn, and sometimes vicious. For them Kings and Queens and their concubines, statesmen and politicians, were fair game for virulent ridicule.

Rushton has been working in the traditional, uncompromising mould almost in isolation – so his shafts have seemed yet more barbed.

In an age when the merest suggestion that our leaders occasionally lapse is to invite something nasty through the letterbox, we are clearly in danger of losing a sense of proportion and need a professional deflater. And a laugh.

Rushton provides the pin, and the grin.   *Nicky Bird, V&A*

CONTENTS

INTRODUCTION

Under 'Profession' in my Passport, I have always put 'Actor/Cartoonist'. My theory is that any job I do *without* a pen in my hand is acting or thereabouts, while any penmanship I do usually involves drawing – even if it's an attempt on the Great Novel (viz *W. G. Grace's Last Case* Methuen. 288 pages and 24 illustrations) I still consider it more a very, very long caption than literature. Now, over the years, this passport has been presented to Immigration Officials of every colour, class, creed and sex, and whereas you might suppose they would light with more excitement on the Actor and look to me for a burst of *Hamlet* or some Rodgers and Hammerstein on the Baggage Carousel, funnily enough, it is always the Cartoonist of whom they seek to know more.

This I find rather touching as it was my chosen profession in the first place, once I had decided that I was not designed by Mother Nature to sit behind a desk in pin-stripes. You know where you are with a Cartoonist. As the passport does not allow you to bill yourself as William "Gay Quips and Dizzy Feet" Rushton, you don't know where you are with the Actor. But the cartoonist, quite obviously, does drawings of a humorous nature. He does not do Sistine Chapels or Studies of Green-Faced Oriental Women, or water-colours of the Lake District or Weeping Clowns. He lives, in the main, by small black-and-white drawings with or without wording. It's as near as you can get to being a Vaudevilleian without leaving your room. In fact, they are a lovely breed. I've only ever met them 'en masse' once when covering a Cartoonists' Conference at a Butlin's Holiday in North Wales for *What the Papers Say*. They wept like babies at the sheer joy of meeting their peers, of meeting anybody.

It is a solitary existence, there in your garret with paper and pens and thumb-lashed edition of *The Writers' and Artists' Year Book*, working through it alphabetically trying to think of Accountancy jokes for *Accountants' World* or fishing gags for *The Anglers' Monthly*. I used to idly jest that *Private Eye* was forged from the mashed pulp of our rejection slips. But, by Heaven, it has its rewards. I received a letter about a year ago from Daar-Es-Salaam asking if *William Rushton's Dirty Book* (which came out in 1962 and was a collection of cartoons to date) was still in print as the last copy in Africa, and that was a photostat, had finally fallen apart. Apparently the book had done the rounds of African Universities for years. It makes your belly swell with pride.

This book is really the result of almost 47 years constant doodling. I have always drawn as long as I can remember. In exercise books, text books, telephone books, all over the *Radio Times*. I worked for a year for a solicitor's firm in the City and in the bowels of their office there are still apparently pink-ribboned deeds covered in shouting Majors and hysterical Conservatives. I always specialised in faces, invariably men of a certain age with massive gin-filled noses, wild moustaches, and deeply bagged eyes.

Tired of soliciting, I decided to throw it all in and embark on the life of a Cartoonist. Briefly I served under Michael Foot on *Tribune* but he was looking for another Vicky, not surprisingly, and I wasn't. I couldn't label clouds 'deflation' or elephants 'inflation'. Still he recommended me to a friend at Harrap and I got a couple of children's books to illustrate. I also became Political Cartoonist of *The Liberal News* where I ran a strip-cartoon called "Brimstone Belcher" who was a Fleet Street journalist in the Chapman Pincher/Sefton Delmer mould. It was finally withdrawn due to public incomprehension, but I was very fond of him. He had a tame 'Yeti' and knew everybody.

Then, in the foulness of time, came *Private Eye*. The major problem was having to devise the lay out which has been likened to a Betting-Shop Floor, but once described to my eternal joy as "Neo-Brechtian Nihilism." One advantage I had was that any gaps in the page could be instantly filled with a cartoon, usually of vastly fat and naked people failing to get it together. (Not now, Doctor Freud).

Looking back at these pictures, I realise that drawing is probably the only thing I have ever done at which I've improved. God knows, there's still room for further, but it's quite cheering. At the same time it now takes longer, but isn't that true of life?

Nowadays for the technically minded I use a *Pentel Ceranomatic* at 0.25, which is why it takes so long. I cross-hatch, where I used to whack black on with a thick brush. For colour I tend to lean towards *Pantones* by *Letraset*, felt nibs both thick and thin and ideal for the man who faced with a paint-box can only come up with shades of brown and puce.

Finally I would like to dedicate these 24 pictures which have fallen out of me over the past couple of years to those I have loved and to whom I owe various debts (How to draw feet, etc). Influences, you might say, but I wouldn't like anyone to feel responsible.

Ronald Searle, George Belcher, Wally Fawkes (Trog), Peter Arno, Pont, Fougasse, Nicholas Bentley, Illingworth, Saul Steinberg, Carl Giles, Bill Tidy and B. Kliban. To Richard Ingrams, my distinguished successor as Editor of the Eye for still employing me and to Bron Waugh for inspiring a fortnightly supply of good old-fashioned Bad Taste. And to my wife Dorgan and son Toby who keep me on track, and at the same time constantly suggest fresh ones.

God save Victoria and Albert.   *Willie Rushton*

Great Moments of History

No. 1
VICTORIA & ALBERT

Given that the V&A are forking out for this one and gathering some of my works into their vaults, (Hello, Posterity, still there are you?) after which really the only decent thing to do is die, I thought the least I could do was to raise my hat to the eponymous Victoria & Albert. The main attraction of these two in my view is that they were clearly crazy about each other, and it showed, despite the fact that it was the Victorian Age (as its name suggests), that she was a Queen and he was German. For that reason it seems boring to have cast Anna Neagle, Anton Walbrook and the like as them over the years, when it was obviously a job for Fred Astaire and Ginger Rogers. Here I have tried to redress the balance.

1.

2.

3.

4.

5.

Victoria & Albert

6.

7.

8.

Great Moments of History

No. 2
VICTORIA AND HER CATS

It would have been laughably easy to have surrounded her with Corgis. No, it wouldn't. I can't draw Corgis. I'm also very bad at cars and trees. Horses too are more trouble than they're worth. Anyway, I'm a cat-fancier. We have three at home, who are all in there somewhere. Cats I have found over the years are infinitely more intelligent than dogs and indeed horses. Try and saddle a cat. They refuse to look like their owners, and live lives of cosy self-indulgence. Gerard de Nerval, famed French loonie, was asked why he was dragging a lobster through the Bois de Boulogne on a length of pink ribbon. "It does not bark" he replied "and knows the secrets of the sea". The same goes for a good cat save that, I fancy, it knows everything.

*Great
Moments
of
History*

No. 3
THE OPENING OF THE GREAT EXHIBITION

Here are V&A again. Though, tell the truth, the person to whom this picture is dedicated is the Chinaman, an involuntary gate-crasher. There was an American who used to gate-crash professionally and appears in many formal photographs of Presidential functions and the like, and there was an Englishman who year after year led in the winner of the Grand National, until betrayed by BBC Television. The Chinaman, however, achieved the highest distinction by appearing in the Official Oil-Painting of the Opening along with the Crowned Heads and Assorted Nobs. He was the Captain of a visiting junk or lugger, who spoke no English and was therefore unable to tell anyone that he was not, in fact, the Emperor of China. Suffice to say, he was for a day and was clearly quite good enough. God Bless him.

The Opening of the Great Exhibition 1851.

Great Moments of History

No. 4
OUR BRAVE FALKLANDS

I did this one immediately after the beastly business in the South Atlantic (a severe case of Prime Ministerial Tension in my book) as a tribute to the Honest Squaddie. I was a Trooper for two years, holding back the Russian hordes, but defending the Falklands must be the worst job in Military History. (What about (a) The Retreat from Moscow? (b) Custer's Last Stand? Discuss.) Catterick was bad enough, but Port Stanley, I ask you. My only contribution to the amusement of that poor, beleaguered garrison, has been to send at the request of a cook ('going slowly mad') a lengthy poem in praise of the Army Catering Corps. That this might save his sanity says something awful about the place. I think we should also give Gibraltar back to the Spanish. There you are, controversy yet.

No. 5
GREAT MOMENTS IN THE HISTORY OF M.G.M.

This was inspired by a photograph in the *Sunday Times* Colour Supplement of the historical moment when Leo, the M.G.M. lion, was filmed doing his impersonation of the Gainsborough Lady or the J. Arthur Rank gong-smiter. This was the inspiration of M.G.M.'s Public Relations Chief, Howard Dietz, (who was also a fine lyricist, and wrote the words of *I Guess I'll Have to Change my Plan*, the best song ever written). It gave me an opportunity to capture a few of my Hollywood favourites (though, actually, Charlie Chaplin never was, and Shirley Temple is only there because I imagine W. C. Fields always wanted to kill her). Bottom left are Harry Langdon and Veronica Lake. I liked them.

Great Moments of History

No. 6
THE 1923 BRITISH EVEREST EXPEDITION PREPARE

Despite a life-long martyrdom to vertigo and never the slightest urge to be a Mountaineer, I have always been fascinated by Everest and stories of it. It's rather less fascinating nowadays as there is a Cook's Tour to Camp Six with an optional Awayday to the Summit. But I remember reading of a man called Wilson who elected to crash a small aeroplane as near to the top as possible and walk up from there. He was never heard of again. And there were numerous British Expeditions when decent chaps with pipes and sensible moustaches would have a crack at it without oxygen or Burberrys. I still like to think that Irvine and Mallory made it in their pork-pie hats and college scarves. The expedition portrayed here is fictional, I admit.

The 1923 British Everest Expedition Prepare.

South Col

Camp One

Johnny Sherpa.

Base Camp.

Great Moments of History

No. 7
AN EXCHANGE OF PICTURES BETWEEN PRESIDENT THEODORE ROOSEVELT AND MR. H. HOUDINI

Two fairly eccentric Americans. In all honesty, I have no idea how this picture came about. I must have started in the middle with Young Roosevelt, a striking figure, and surrounded him with the things he seemed to be most famous for killing – Cubans and Teddy Bears. Then I found a photograph of the Old Roosevelt and tossed that in. The mystery for once is How did Houdini get *in*? Picasso said something like "Great Art is usually the result of an accident". Heaven knows I'm not Picasso but thanks anyway, Pablo, I think you speak for all of us.

Great
Moments
of
History

No. 8
A TRIBUTE TO THOMAS EDISON

This is a memoir of a brief holiday in Fort Myers, Florida. The main claim to fame of Fort Myers is that it houses the Winter Home of Thomas Edison. His original light-bulb still burns there. In the garden he grew almost everything, but was most interested in Bamboo. He thought this was the answer to the filament. It wasn't, of course, a fact which makes me feel a lot brighter. After all you might have been there when he was wrestling with filament, and you'd have said "Have you tried bamboo, Tom?" and there are those who would have scoffed.

Great Moments of History

No. 9
EDWARD VIII IN NEW YORK CITY

My wife and I once wrote a musical about Edward VIII. (Never yet performed but still in the cupboard, Mr Merrick). The whole Abdication business always struck us as more Musical Comedy than Drama. Another job for Fred and Ginger. An American Queen would have been a tremendous asset. Then again I always thought Prince Charles would have struck a blow for something else, had he married the Three Degrees.

THE ROOMS OF
Mr & Mrs ERNEST SIMPSON.

THE VISIT OF H.R.H THE PRINCE OF
WALES TO NEW YORK CITY.
1933.

Great
Moments
of
History

No. 10
TAXIDERMY

This started with the two gentlemen playing cards in the middle, who I found in a book about the Raj. Then I indulged myself in mandrills and tapirs and the like. I imagine that they are Endangered Species, most species are. The two gentlemen bottom right are in fact dressed for some religious outing in Madeira, but I threw them in on the grounds that a keen taxidermist will stuff anything that has stopped moving.

Have YOU Considered a Fulfilling Career in TAXIDERMY?

_Great
Moments
of
History_

No. 11
BRUSH UP YOU PIDGIN

Dorgan, my wife, wrote an excellent Pidgin-English Phrase Book for Collins. She is Australian and many of her relatives worked in or visited New Guinea. It's a wonderful language and a good deal more comprehensible and poetic than Esperanto. It was Princess Anne no less who told me that a helicopter was "Mixmaster him belong Jesus Christ". You can see I meet a lot of interesting people in my line of work.

On the First of May 1933 Nicholas and Daphne Coffin set out from Ruislip on an Epic Journey into the Wilds of New Guinea to write a Pidgin-English Phrase-Book. Their subsequent disappearance in the Jungle of New Britain created a Mystery that has baffled Literati ever since ....

Brush up your Pidgin

DORGAN RUSHTON

A Sensible, Conversational Beginner's Phrase-Book of Pidgin-English (Pisin-Inglis) for the British Traveller, including an Everyday Guide to SURVIVAL in the Jungles of New Guinea, New Britain, New Ireland, the Bismarck Archipelago, the New Hebrides, the Louisiade Archipelago, New Caledonia, the Solomons, Fiji and the Loyalty Islands. The Only Phrase-Book in the World with a VIOLENT ENDING

Great Moments of History

No. 12
EDWARD VII DOWN UNDER

This one is also dedicated to my wife – I love a Sun-burnt-Woman. This is a Town like Alice – but not exactly. Many a good time I've enjoyed in Australia, indeed I was married there under what turned out to be Methodist Rules in Crow's Nest, a suburb of Sydney. The outback is never far away. Buy a road-map of New South Wales and half of it is almost plain white. The odd track is drawn in dotted lines to represent its frailty, and usually accompanied by the legend "Forget it". If you're still looking for the Lost Tribe of Israel, try Australia.

*Great
Moments
of
History*

No. 13
THE STATUE OF LIBERTY

Such was the thoroughness of Signor Bartholdi who designed her
using his rather brutish-looking mother as model, and Monsieur Eiffel
who engineered her innards, that they erected the whole thing in a
Paris street, prior to sending it to America in 214 crates. I'm not
absolutely certain why a "Crime Passionnelle" has been committed in
the foreground, perhaps I feel you can't really capture the Spirit of Paris
without one.

Great Moments of History

No. 14
CREATING AN UNFORTUNATE PRESIDENT

All right America, yes, this has something to do with Ronald Reagan, although, in my view, more actors should go into politics. We do read the lines better. Even Reagan. Somehow however I can't believe Abraham Lincoln would have cracked it had he been as lousy a lawyer as Reagan was an actor.

Creating an Unfortunate President.

Great Moments of History

No. 15
LES ILES MALHEUREUSES

I think I read somewhere that Devil's Island was about to become a Tourist Paradise. This is the nature of things. One can imagine old lags in a low Parisian Bar looking over green drinks at the old days and sadly mouthing in raw garlic "The developers have ruined it".

Great Moments of History

No. 16
VENEZIA

Sinking it may be under the weight of industrial effluent, tourists and pigeon-lime, but it still does an old heart good to sit in St Mark's square and listen to the various orchestras playing against one another. Sell your mother and go there on the Orient Express. It's one of those rare places that makes you proud to be human. I shall still be visiting it when it's in the sub-basement.

VENEZIA.

Great
Moments
of
History

No. 17
THE MUTANTS AT HOME

World War III seems to be very big at the moment. *The Day After,*
Threads – the long-awaited destruction of Sheffield by the BBC, even
songs by Frankie Goes to Huddersfield and Boy George, who did not
know my Father. A year or so ago *The Observer* conducted a Consumer's
Guide to Fall-Out Shelters. I thought this tasteful study of the Mutants
At Home pointed up some idiocies of the whole horrible business, but
found I had no idea what to put at the top where London or wherever
had once been. "Dinosaurs" said my son, Toby, and damned if I could
think of anything better.

Great Moments of History

No. 18
BEYOND THE PALE

There's something peculiarly daunting about those old Victorian school-buildings, so I weaved one into a Moral Tale, A Warning to Victorian Progeny. I like to think the lad overcame this early setback and went on to become Chairman of the Conservative Party or such. I always think it says a lot for education that Noel Coward left school at nine.

BEYOND THE PALE

Great Moments of History

No. 19
NOTRE DAME v. NEW YORK YANKEES

Any excuse, however feeble, to have a go at Quasimodo. Who wants to draw Robert Redford, when you can go mad with rotten teeth, warts and a good hump? But then I'd rather do a Study of Urban Blight than ever have painted *The Hay Wain* with all those bloody trees. Also, Early Baseball players are quite as picturesque as Early Cricketers, if not more so.

*Great
Moments
of
History*

No. 20
THE ADORATION OF THE MAGGIE

This one I did for *Private Eye* who, in my view, printed it far too small — it would have been a double-page spread in the good old days when I was Art Editor. Actually, I think it looks better here in colour. This is quite an accurate reproduction of her birth place in Grantham, where the trouble started. Unfortunately, you cannot run a country on the same lines as a Victorian Grocery, try as you may.

Great Moments of History

No. 21
THE ASCENT OF WALT WHITMAN

Why not? I only say that once because almost invariably those I've shown this picture to, smile and nod, and then say 'Why'? It's at times like those that I realise I am a cartoonist and not an artist. Nobody ever stood behind Picasso at work and said "I don't like that eye" or "What is it?" or "Why"? They'll stand behind a cartoonist and say "The nose is too long" or "Is that a moustache?" for hours on end. Why not? I liked the look of Walt Whitman, and the rest is History.

Do I contradict myself?
Very well then I contradict myself,
(I am large,
I contain multitudes).
Song of Myself.

The Ascent of Walt Whitman.

*Great
Moments
of
History*

No. 22
THE M.C.C. AT THE KREMLIN

Before you dismiss this as a foolish dream of a middle-aged loonie, remember that no two Cricketing countries have ever gone to war. (All right, India v Pakistan, but there's no point in dramatic generalisation, if you're going to pick hairs). Perhaps it would be more practical if the Russians took up Baseball, but they're flirting with Tennis, and should they take up Cricket it would in my view make for an altogether better world.

Great
Moments
of
History

No. 23
CHARIOTS OF GIN

An antidote to the current frenzy for Health Food and Jogging. It is my firm belief that nowadays more people are being buried in track-suits than shrouds. I did this during the LA Olympics and somehow it made me feel much better at 3 o'clock in the morning.

Great
Moments
of
History

No. 24
MOUNT RUSHTON

This is pure self-indulgence. The luxury item I asked Roy Plomley for on *Desert Island Discs* was a set of ever-sharp chisels so that I could slowly convert my island into a vast sculpture on the Mount Rushmore principle. Then I drew a rough design, couldn't think what to put at the bottom, so inserted myself with detonator as if to atone. A clapped-out Britannia and John Bull seem pleased.

Mount Rushton.